Sections

CW00508075

Purpose of the book

The purpose of this book is to demystify the Phonics Screening Check and equip you with the knowledge and tools to effectively support your child's phonics development.

Phonics Screening Check Quick Guide for Parents

This book has been designed to provide you with a comprehensive understanding of the Phonics Screening Check and empower you to support your child's reading journey. As a parent, you play a crucial role in helping your child develop strong phonics skills, which are fundamental for early reading success.

The Phonics Screening Check is an important assessment conducted in Year 1 to evaluate your child's phonics knowledge and decoding skills. It consists of a set of 40 words, including both real words and pseudo (nonsense) words. Real words are familiar words found in everyday reading, while pseudo words are made-up words that assess a child's ability to apply phonics skills.

Screening Check Explained

Format

The check is usually conducted on a one-to-one basis, allowing the teacher or teaching assistant to gauge your child's phonics progress individually. It helps identify any areas of difficulty or gaps in their phonics knowledge, ensuring that targeted support can be provided to help them overcome challenges and improve their reading abilities.

By familiarizing yourself with the Phonics Screening Check, you will be better prepared to support your child's learning journey.

Understanding Phonics

Phonics and its role in reading

Phonics is an instructional method that teaches the relationship between sounds (phonemes) and the written letters or letter combinations (graphemes) that represent those sounds. It is the foundation upon which children build their reading skills.

Phonics instruction helps children understand the sound-symbol correspondence, enabling them to recognize and decode words accurately.

By learning phonics, children develop the ability to break down words into individual sounds and blend those sounds together to form words. This decoding process allows them to read words they have not encountered before, expanding their reading vocabulary and comprehension. Phonics also enhances spelling skills, as children learn to segment words into sounds and match them with the appropriate letters.

Phonemes (individual sounds) and Graphemes (letter representations)

Phonemes are the smallest units of sound in a language. In English, we have approximately 44 phonemes, such as /s/, /a/, /t/, /p/, and /ee/. These phonemes can be combined to form words.

For example, the word "cat" is composed of three phonemes: /k/ /æ/ /t/. Understanding phonemes is vital for children as it enables them to decode and encode words accurately.

Graphemes, on the other hand, are the written representations of phonemes. They can be single letters (such as "s" or "m") or combinations of letters (such as "ch" or "sh") that represent specific sounds. Graphemes provide a visual link to the sounds in words. Learning the correspondence between phonemes and graphemes helps children connect the dots between spoken and written language.

PHONICS SCREENING CHECK
Format and Structure

The Phonics Screening Check is a short, one-to-one assessment conducted with your child's teacher or a teaching assistant. It typically takes place in Year 1 and aims to evaluate your child's phonics knowledge and decoding skills. The check consists of a set of 40 words, divided into two sections.

1. The first section contains a series of real words. These are familiar words found in everyday reading and have meaningful context. They may include words such as "cat," "ship," or "rain." The purpose of this section is to assess your child's ability to accurately decode and read words that they are likely to encounter in their reading materials.

2. The second section consists of pseudo (nonsense) words which follow phonics rules, but they do not carry any meaning. E.g. your child may come across words like "frib," "shoom," or "bront." This allows the assessment to focus on your child's phonics skills rather than their sight word recognition. It helps evaluate their ability to apply phonics knowledge and sound out unfamiliar words.

During the check, your child will be asked to read each word aloud. Both the real words and pseudo words are presented in isolation without any surrounding text. This isolates the decoding skill and allows the assessor to evaluate your child's ability to apply phonics rules independently.

It's important to note that the pseudo words are not intended to be real words, so your child should not worry about their meaning. Encourage them to focus on applying their phonics knowledge, blending the sounds together, and reading the words as accurately as possible.

Scoring and Assessment Process

THE PHONICS SCREENING CHECK

☐ is not a test that your child can pass or fail. Instead, it provides valuable information about their progress in phonics and identifies any areas that may need additional support.

EACH WORD

☐ in the check is assigned a score of either 'correct' or 'incorrect' based on your child's pronunciation and decoding accuracy. The scores are then tallied to determine their overall performance. The results are often shared with parents to provide insight into their child's phonics development.

Scoring and Assessment Process

IT'S IMPORTANT

☐ to remember that the Phonics Screening Check is just one snapshot of your child's reading abilities. It is not meant to be a comprehensive assessment of their overall literacy skills. If your child requires additional support, their teacher or school may provide targeted interventions and strategies to help them progress.

Preparing for the Phonics Screening Check

1. Supporting your child's phonics development at home

1. Create a print-rich environment: Surround your child with letters, words, and books. Label objects around the house, display alphabet charts, and have a variety of age-appropriate books available. This exposure to print reinforces their understanding of letter-sound relationships and builds vocabulary.

2. Read aloud together: Regularly read books aloud with your child, focusing on stories that contain phonic patterns. Encourage them to actively listen for sounds and engage in discussions about the story. This helps develop their phonemic awareness and comprehension skills.

3. Encourage daily practice: Set aside a dedicated time each day for phonics practice. Keep sessions short and engaging to maintain your child's interest. Consistency is key, so make it a regular part of your routine.

2. Phonics activities and games to practice sound recognition and blending

1. Sound scavenger hunt: Go on a hunt around your home or outside to find objects that start with specific sounds. Encourage your child to identify the initial sounds of objects and match them to the corresponding letters.

2.   Sound sorting: Create a set of picture cards representing different objects or animals. Ask your child to sort the cards based on their initial or ending sounds. This activity strengthens their ability to recognize and categorize sounds.

3.   Word building: Provide letter cards or magnetic letters and encourage your child to build words by blending the sounds together. Start with simple CVC (consonant-vowel-consonant) words like "cat" or "dog" and gradually progress to more complex words.

3. Resources and websites for further practice

1.   Online phonics games and apps: There are various interactive resources available online that provide engaging phonics activities. Websites like PhonicsPlay, Teach Your Monster to Read, and ABCmouse offer games, exercises, and interactive lessons for phonics practice.

2.   Phonics books and workbooks: Explore a range of phonics books and workbooks designed for children at your child's reading level. Look for titles that incorporate phonics patterns and provide opportunities for reading practice.

3.   Local library resources: Visit your local library and explore their collection of phonics books, CDs, and educational resources. Librarians can also provide recommendations for age-appropriate materials.

Phonics Screening Practice List

Real words

chill	start
blank	phone
scribe	grit
whisk	shin
dentist	gang

Real words

pound	clown
slide	brick
drift	newt
mixer	jazz
chain	light

Nonsense Alien Words

dox	smeck
yoop	glisp
lazz	blies
chirt	blate
jimp	olf

Nonsense Alien Words

steck	bin
voo	ulf
blurst	spron
quemp	geck
gild	vap

Real words

starling	week
day	hooks
slide	strap
newt	trains
finger	cap

drak	crept
fuel	feeling
thump	haystack
squawk	morning
stroke	drank

Nonsense Alien
Words

scroy	spreet
melp	jigh
faum	shound
frue	cripe
quipe	thoft

Nonsense Alien
Words

chom	jound
snemp	blan
tord	tox
fape	stroft
thazz	terg

in

at

beg

sum

Alien words practice

ot

vap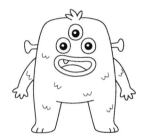

osk

ect

Phonics Screening Previous Years' Assessments

2022
Assessment

bem

dax

kig

eld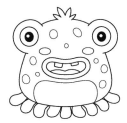

besh

quab

barp

chell

grux

smung

nesk

foint

thud

hang

coin

shell

twig

flick

vest

horns

vair

cloat

tirt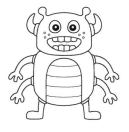

whike

plunt

flards

spran

splew

globe

teams

bowl

chase

print

clouds

spree

stroke

visit

fabric

trapeze

concrete

2019
Assessment

sut

yad

dop

uct

meck

shig

joil

chort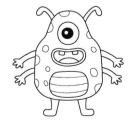

blem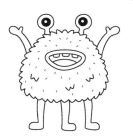

drell

fusp

quisk

shop

yell

peel

check

plug

sweep

soft

yards

vaw

meast

waib

zome

brend

throst

stret

spraw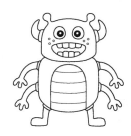

few

fried

beak

cute

crust

trails

strip

scraps

label

vanish

blossom

thankful

2018
Assessment

reb

wup

jub

eps

vuss

quop

zook

chack

skap

blorn

meft

veems

chop

sing

dart

shock

flat

skill

gift

coins

var

slirt

weaf

pobe

flisp

braint

scrid

splote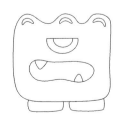

twice

gloom

turn

mode

blast

groans

spray

strike

delay

modern

saucers

charming

2017
Assessment

dat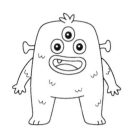

cag

rin

ept

jash

quib

coid

quass

glog

blard

disp

murbs

chum

kick

reef

short

blot

greet

dust

parks

tay

sloam

zued

meve

clend

brait

scrug

splue

feast

goal

shape

trunk

groups

straw

scribe

model

person

chapter

reptiles

Additional reading materials for parents who want to explore further

THE BOOK OF SOUNDS

- [ ] First Phonics Dictionary focusing on Digraphs by Amayo Chioms. Beautifully illustrated home and school reference tool which supports the teaching of reading and spelling by gathering all the digraphs of the English language in one book

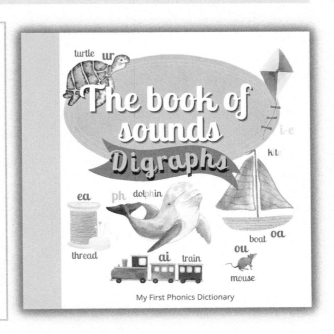

RAISING KIDS WHO READ

- [ ] "Raising Kids Who Read: What Parents and Teachers Can Do" by Daniel T. Willingham: Discusses the science behind reading acquisition and provides practical advice for parents to support their child's reading development.

Printed in Great Britain
by Amazon

37118138R00044